T0170117

FIGURES IN CHINA'S SPACE INDUSTRY

Who is Feng Ru?

www.royalcollins.com

FIGURES IN CHINA'S SPACE INDUSTRY

Who is Feng Ru?

By Ye Qiang and Dong Pingping

Books Beyond Boundaries

ROYAL COLLINS

On January 12, 1884, Feng Ru was born to a peasant family in Xingpu village, Enping District, Canton. It was a difficult time when China, under the imperial Qing Dynasty government, was under foreign attack during the Sino-French War.

When Feng Ru was young and studying in traditional private schools, his teacher not only taught him knowledge from textbooks but also stories from fiction. The great battle of Xin Huan and Thunder Boy flying in the air in *The Canonization of the Gods* was his favorite. Descriptions such as "four pairs of wings are seen in heaven, wind and thunder are heard resounding" were so fascinating that they kept young Feng Ru wondering about these beautiful stories of flying all day long.

In 1895, at the age of 11, Feng Ru boarded an ocean liner and traveled to study in the United States.

In the US, after a few years of study in school and in factories, Feng Ru mastered skills and techniques related to mechanics and electrical appliances. He was able to design and build all kinds of machines. The small alternator he invented was both easy to use and easy to carry around. The piling machine and the water pump he designed were low in price but high in quality and received a good public reputation. At the time, countries such as Germany, France, and the US had all attempted to bring short flight to reality with flying machines such as the hang glider, and some had established aviation conferences. At the same time, there were also many scientists who held skeptical and opposing ideas about flying. For example, Lord Kelvin, who is regarded as the "father of thermodynamics," refused an invitation from the aviation conference in 1896 and said: "I don't believe in anything in air travel other than an air balloon." But Feng Ru was different from those skeptics. He showed great interest in this new idea of airplanes–flying machines heavier than air.

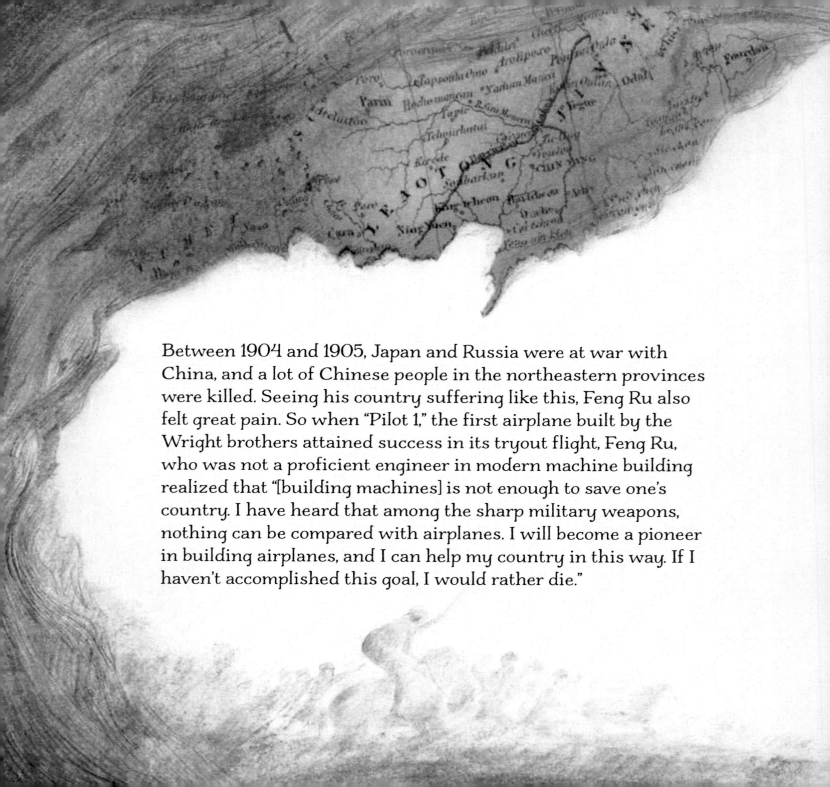

Between 1904 and 1905, Japan and Russia were at war with China, and a lot of Chinese people in the northeastern provinces were killed. Seeing his country suffering like this, Feng Ru also felt great pain. So when "Pilot 1," the first airplane built by the Wright brothers attained success in its tryout flight, Feng Ru, who was not a proficient engineer in modern machine building realized that "[building machines] is not enough to save one's country. I have heard that among the sharp military weapons, nothing can be compared with airplanes. I will become a pioneer in building airplanes, and I can help my country in this way. If I haven't accomplished this goal, I would rather die."

With that said, Feng Ru has made a resolution as a young man—
to build planes for his own country and to defend it from outside
bullies.

9

In 1906, Feng Ru travelled from New York to San Francisco as a reputable engineer. He refused to work in a Chinese company and decided to contribute his strength to his far away country. He said to his assistant Zhu Zhuquan: "The war between Japan and Russia was dangerous for our country. At this time of combat and competition, airplanes are the most important in an army. Instead of spending several millions on building a battleship, why not use this money to build planes which are cheap and easy to make, and we can have several hundred of them. If we could have a thousand planes to guard the Chinese ports, the interior would be safe."

Several donors were willing to help Feng Ru with his dream:
Huang Qi, Zhang Nan, and Tan Yaoneng. With their support,
Feng Ru got around 1,000 dollars and rented a small workshop
in Oakland, California, which then turned into the first Chinese
airplane factory—the Canton manufacturing machine factory.
There, Feng Ru wholeheartedly began to build airplanes.

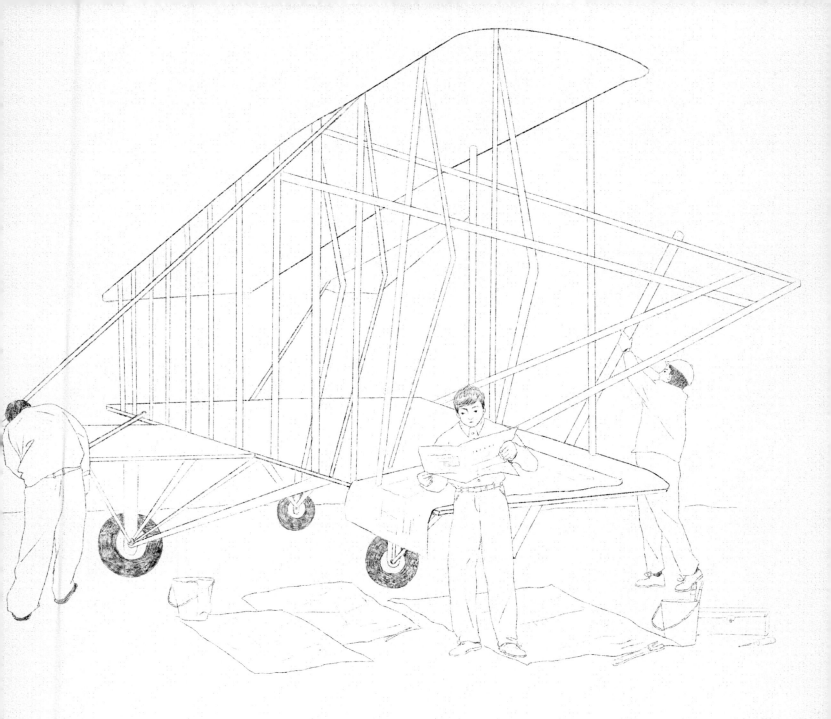

At the time, all information about building planes was blocked by western countries, so it was very difficult for Feng Ru and his team to do their job. They had to rely on themselves to learn about aerodynamics and to draw blueprints. After trying for two years, on the evening of September 21, 1909, "Feng Ru I" succeeded in her flight test and showed wonderful features during the flight. News about this was reported both in China and in other countries. Feng Ru, with his photo on the front page of the *San Francisco Examiner*, was praised as the "Oriental Wright Brother," followed by the comment: "Chinese have beaten the whites in the field of aviation!"

CHINESE LEAVES WHITES BEHIND IN AVIATION

Oakland Genius Makes First Flight on Coast in Craft Driven by Home-Made Motor

TRIAL ENDS IN MISHAP

Fung Joe Guey Comes Down With Crash, but Unhurt; Will Make New Ship for Cantonese

Only Chinese See Flight

ORIENTAL WRIGHT SOA
BIPLANE HOMEMADE CRAF

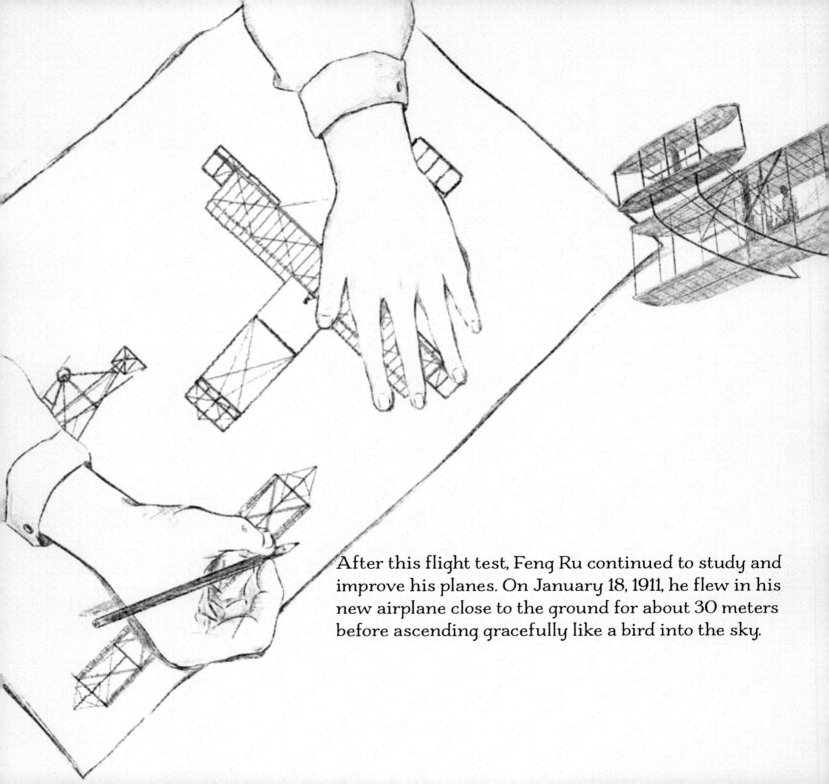

After this flight test, Feng Ru continued to study and improve his planes. On January 18, 1911, he flew in his new airplane close to the ground for about 30 meters before ascending gracefully like a bird into the sky.

Later, Feng Ru also consistently improved the details of his planes and came up with the final version of "Feng Ru II." It reached a speed of 105 km per hour, a distance of 32 km, and a height of 215 meters.

In February 1911, Feng Ru returned to China with his three assistants, Zhu Zhuquan, Situ Biru, and Zhu Zhaohuai, as well as their equipment and two airplanes (one was not fully finished). In order to help the people understand aviation and to inspire them to support Chinese aviation development, Feng Ru started to do public flying shows. In April 1912, Feng Ru was doing a public flying show in Canton, and this was the first time that a Chinese person flew over his country's territory in his own plane.

On the hot summer day of August 25, 1912, Feng Ru did his last flying show.

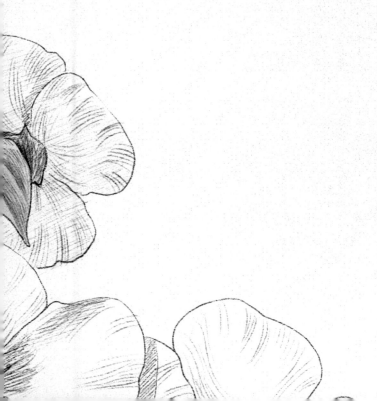

He was wearing his flying cap, windproof goggles, and long boots. After he introduced to the audience how an airplane functions, how it was built, and how to pilot it, he took off. He ascended elegantly into the air and showed his flexible flying positions, which greatly excited the audience. Then, Feng Ru wanted to pull the airplane a little higher but he lost control, probably because he moved too fast or that the airflow was unstable. He dropped and crashed onto the lawn. When he was rescued from the wreckage of the plane, Feng Ru was badly injured. He was rushed to the hospital, but it was too late, and he died there at the age of 29.

Throughout his young life, Feng Ru closely connected his destiny with that of his country. Even under the pressure of a shortage of money and the inaccessibility of technical support, he still tried his best to design and build airplanes. He devoted his whole life to this career.

Feng Ru once said, "I want to rescue my people from their suffering so much; more than anything else, I wish to save my country from collapsing." All men are without exception responsible for their country's fate. Harboring the dream of "empowering my country, saving our rights," Feng Ru will always shine through the history of Chinese manned powered flight with his outstanding efforts and contributions.

About the Authors

YE QIANG studied oil painting at Sichuan Fine Arts Institute. After graduating in 2001, he continued to teach in the Institute until 2008. Since then, he's been teaching as an Associate Professor in the Department of New Media Art and Design at Beihang University (Beijing University of Aeronautics and Astronautics). Ye's paintings have been displayed in hundreds of national and international exhibitions, and he has held solo exhibitions in galleries, including the Shanghai Art Museum, six times. Ye's paintings and scholarship can be found in more than 20 academic journals and monographs, such as *Art Observation, Art China, History to Chinese Oil Painting*, and more. He has also published seven textbooks, including *Basic Techniques in Drawing, Basic Techniques in Coloring*, and *A Brief Introduction in Abstract Painting Languages*.

DONG PINGPING is Vice-Secretary of the Party Committee and a member of the Supervisory Commission of the Department of New Media Art and Design at Beihang University.

Figures in China's Space Industry:
Who is Feng Ru?

Written by Ye Qiang and Dong Pingping

First published in 2022 by Royal Collins Publishing Group Inc.
Groupe Publication Royal Collins Inc.
BKM Royalcollins Publishers Private Limited

Headquarters: 550-555 boul. René-Lévesque O Montréal (Québec) H2Z1B1 Canada
India office: 805 Hemkunt House, 8th Floor, Rajendra Place, New Delhi 110 008

Original Edition © Shaanxi People's Education Press Co., Ltd.

All rights reserved. Without limiting the rights under copyright reserved above, no part of this publication may be reproduced, stored in or introduced into a retrieval system, or transmitted in any form or by any means (electronic, mechanical, photocopying, recording or otherwise), without the prior written permission of both the copyright owner and the above publisher of this book.

ISBN: 978-1-4878-0893-8

To find out more about our publications, please visit www.royalcollins.com.